Arthur Bennett

Travels in Norway

Arthur Bennett

Travels in Norway

ISBN/EAN: 9783744742108

Printed in Europe, USA, Canada, Australia, Japan

Cover: Foto ©Andreas Hilbeck / pixelio.de

More available books at **www.hansebooks.com**

TRAVELS IN NORWAY;

OR,

THREE WEEKS
IN THE "LAND OF THE MIDNIGHT SUN."

BY

ARTHUR BENNETT.

PUBLISHED FOR THE AUTHOR BY
J. TRUSLOVE, HORSEMARKET STREET,
WARRINGTON.
1879.

PRINTED BY
GRANT AND CO., LONDON.

TRAVELS IN NORWAY.

June 20th, 1879.—Along with a certain gentleman and his son, whom we will call Mr. Saxon and Master Harry Saxon, I left the Central Station, Warrington, at 9.10 a.m., a number of enthusiastic friends attending us to the platform and bidding us "Adieu" in a most pathetic manner. In the carriage we discovered a young farmer who resides in the neighbourhood, and who was convulsed with laughter at our efforts to express ourselves in the Norwegian tongue.

The scenery near Woodhead is superb, a long chain of artificial or semi-artificial lakes which constitute the water supply of Manchester running parallel with the railway for several miles. These lakes have been formed by filling up valleys, and then collecting in them all the water which flows from the surrounding hills. As you ascend, the level of each lake is higher than that of its predecessor. In one of them rises a huge object, somewhat resembling that remarkable obelisk, Cleopatra's Needle, but which I understand is a huge factory chimney, which was left standing when the valley was submerged. Soon afterwards the line passes through one of the longest tunnels in England. We were in darkness for exactly five minutes. Having emerged we noticed that streams now took an eastern direction, in their way to the German Ocean.

Passing through Barnsley we arrived at Doncaster, celebrated for its races, and were much interested in contemplating a castle,* which stood near the line upon a slight eminence, and which, Mr. Saxon informed me, was the scene of many of the thrilling incidents narrated in Scott's masterpiece, "Ivanhoe." Acquaintance with history, &c., adds greatly to one's enjoyment, for if we had not been aware of this fact the castle would have been to us simply a block of antique architecture.

Somewhere in this neighbourhood a rather eccentric-looking personage, with sandy whiskers and moustache, entered our compartment. He amused me greatly, for he put all the fingers of one hand in his mouth, and leaned in a corner against the window, whilst his countenance bore a most puzzled expression, as if he were trying to solve a very intricate mathematical problem, and seeking inspiration from the trees and hedges which we rapidly passed. I more than once broke out into a wholly irrepressible peal of laughter, though I took care not to let him know that he was the subject of my mirth. We saw scores of splendid hawthorn bushes in full bloom, from which was emitted a pleasing fragrance.

Goole, the next town of importance through which we passed, seemed to be a fine place, and bore an aspect of cleanliness and order very pleasing to behold. Then that magnificent stretch of water, the Humber, appeared, and a delicious sea breeze was wafted through the open windows of the carriage. Forty-five minutes more and the train rushed into the suburbs of Hull, which are beautiful, and almost immediately drew up at the Paragon Station. Our friend, the farmer, whose destination was Yarmouth, here left us; whilst we entered a cab and drove to the commodious premises of Thomas Wilson, Sons and Co., with the intention of obtaining return tickets to Norway, but were told to get them from the steward on board the "Hero," which steamship was to convey us to Christiania.

After a capital dinner at the Cross Keys Hotel we had a long stroll through Hull, inspecting all objects of interest which we encountered in our journey. Near

---

* Query. Probably Athelstone Tower, a very striking object from the railway.

the Dock Office is erected a lofty column and statue in honour of Wilberforce, that noble hero who fought so well on behalf of the poor, down-trodden, abused, dark-skinned, but yet immortal negro ; and my heart paid a silent tribute to his goodness, whilst I also longed to be able to do something to aggrandize the condition of my fellow-men. How true is that verse in Longfellow's " Psalm of Life :"

> "Lives of great men all remind us
> We can make our lives sublime,
> And departing, leave behind us
> Footprints in the sands of time,"

for as we contemplate the nobility of others a feeling of sterling emulation is aroused in *us*, and *we* long to make "*our* lives sublime."

The Dock Office is a fine building, being surmounted by three domes. Holy Trinity Church is a remarkably large edifice, and is rather tastefully decorated.

I fancy Friday must be the market day in Hull ; for a square in this vicinity was crowded with retailers of all manner of wares and a "Cheap Jack," who made quite an eloquent oration about a twopenny box of ointment, not forgetting to laud his own veracity, sagacity, &c.

We next strolled down to the Humber, and noticed that the colour of its waters was a shade of yellow, or "umber," which suggested to Mr. Saxon the idea that this peculiar tint was the originator of the name.

At about five o'clock we went on board the "Hero," which is by no means a bad steamship. To us was allotted a private cabin, most comfortable. The scene on the quay was interesting, especially near the "Hero," for she was engaged in shipping a cargo of Manchester, Birmingham, and other English goods. The dock hands were paid whilst we lay secured to the quay. The system of payment is a capital one. All the men form in single file, and one by one pass an office, where each, without the slightest confusion being created, receives his money.

Towards seven o'clock the "Hero" was hauled out of dock, and in course of time entered the Humber. She had not proceeded far, however, when a stoppage

was made, the object of which was to await the arrival
of a tug bearing despatches from T. Wilson, Sons
and Co.

But at last we had overcome every hindrance and
were steaming down the Humber, leaving Hull far in
our wake. A bell rang and we descended into the
saloon, where was laid a table of delicacies, including
reindeer tongue, which is superb. There was a strange
assembly gathered round the table, amongst whom
were three pretty ladies, one of whom I learnt was a
Norwegian who had been living in England for fifteen
years. Harry and I afterwards got quite friendly with
her, and gained from her much valuable information
relative to our destination. Next to the ladies, for of
course they always have the greatest influence upon
gentlemen, I was most struck by a reverend-looking
gentleman, with white hair, grey beard, and exceedingly
"meek and mild" countenance. He was a Norwegian;
but I designated him "the Swiss clergyman"—why, I
can't tell you, for I'm sure I don't know.

We paced the deck until the "glimmering landscape"
gradually "faded from our view" and night began to
throw her pall over land and sea. Just before we left
the Humber we descried the town of Grimsby, in Lin-
colnshire, in which was conspicuous a huge pile, which
I couldn't make into anything but a monument, but
which, I afterwards learnt, is a hydraulic column.

On Spurn Head, the last point we saw, glistened a
most brilliant light, which, I suppose, proceeded from a
lighthouse.

We were now out " on the ocean." As we left the
land behind I thought of Byron's lines :—

> "*I* tuned *my* farewell in the dim twilight,
>   While flew the vessel on her snowy wing,
> And fleeting shores receded from *my* sight,
>   Thus to the elements *I* poured *my* last 'Good Night :'

> " Adieu, adieu ! my native shore
>   Fades o'er the waters blue ;
>   The night-winds sigh, the breakers roar,
>   And shrieks the wild sea-mew.

Yon sun that sets upon the sea
We *leave him* in his flight;
Farewell awhile to him and thee,
My native land—Good Night!"

For a long time Harry and I rambled about the deck,
scrutinised the engine, funnels, ventilators, anchors,
shrouds, belaying pins, capstan, compass, rudder, and
all the other requisites of a steamer; and gazed intently
at a fleet of fishing boats which lay off the Dogger
Bank, near which congregate, I believe, innumerable
hosts of fish. The lamps were now ignited; that on the
starboard side being green, and that on the larboard or
port side red. We saw a person whom we thought we
recognised beneath the lights, went to him, and discovered that he was none other than our railway companion, the renowned finger-biter and problem-solver.
A conversation ensued, from which we learnt that he
was a Norwegian, and captain of a vessel trading off
the coast of Norway.

After considerable deliberation, for such portentous
decisions cannot be arrived at without deliberation, we
resolved to go to bed.

June 21st.—At 5 a.m. I awoke in a peculiar state
of mind. My bump of locality must have been dis-
organized, for I had not the slightest idea as to my
whereabouts. I could hear a great noise overhead as
of huge waves sweeping across the deck, and then my
thoughts began to assume their wonted sway. "I
must be on the sea," I reasoned, "and surely a terrible
storm is raging." I heard the noise of the engines, and
it suddenly occurred to me that I was on my way to
Norway. This opinion was confirmed the next instant,
for a slipper was hurled at me from the opposite berth,
my companion's merry face appearing the moment after.
I was told that he hadn't been asleep during the whole
night except for about an hour.

We rose, had coffee, and went on deck, where we
were greeted by several gentlemen who had arrived
there before us, and where I·learnt that the noise which
I had taken for waves sweeping across the vessel was

but the sound caused by the sailors who were washing the deck.

Nothing of very great importance occurred during the day. I spent it in rambling about the deck, reading Marryat's tale, "The King's Own," writing my journal, studying the Norwegian language, and last, and perhaps best of all, in talking to the hereinbefore-mentioned Norwegian lady, who is very nice indeed.

Captain Pepper, the commander of the "Hero," had caused an awning to be erected for the convenience of his two other lady passengers and their cavaliers, whom we afterwards learnt were the Hon. Captain Molyneux, his wife, and two friends, which at dusk was vacated. Harry and I immediately took possession in the name of the Norwegian lady. We made it free from draught and very comfortable, and I assure you the three of us spent a most enjoyable time.

Sunday, June 22nd.—I was roused by Mr. Saxon exclaiming that land was in sight, washed, dressed, and went on deck. To my surprise I found that we were in a land-locked harbour, with a very pretty town, surrounded in most directions by picturesque hills and trees, coming down to the water's edge. In the bay lay several ships at anchor ; and numerous barges, boats, &c., put off in the direction of the "Hero," from the deck of which a splendid view of Christiansand, the town in question, might be obtained ; its white or gray houses, which are mostly built of wood, with red-tiled roofs ; its church, with a peculiarly-shaped tower, and which, I heard, boasts a magnificent band ; its hospital, so prettily situated amid verdant trees ; its quays, and, stretching away behind, a mist-covered hill.

The "Hero" discharged a considerable quantity of her cargo here, which was conveyed in barges to the shore ; and several of her passengers left us, including the "Swiss clergyman." The Norwegian boatmen seemed to be very decent fellows, and I was interested in listening to their conversation, accompanied by corresponding gestures, although they spoke in what was to me almost an unknown tongue.

During breakfast we sailed out of the bay ; and now the ship commenced to roll rather violently. I went on deck with the intention of gazing over the stern ; but I found that it wouldn't do, for the deck seemed to positively go from under my feet, leaving me behind in the air. In consequence of this I strolled, or rather tottered, forwards, ending by nearly tumbling into the arms of my friend, the Norwegian lady. It was raining heavily, but the after part of the deck was covered by an awning ; so I sat by her side for " sobe codsiderable tibe," as Thobas Delolbe says. Harry didn't seem to see the joke, for he went below ; and some time afterwards I found him with a very pale face, and was told that he had been sick !

Mr. Saxon soon had us on deck again, for the swell speedily subsided. We went in the smoke-room, and were quickly occupied in unravelling the mysteries of the Norwegian currency. We were now sailing along the coast in a northerly direction. Harry went for a walk, and the Hon. Captain Molyneux being in the room, Mr. Saxon and I had a conversation with him about Norway. He is an agreeable gentleman ; indeed, so are the majority of the passengers, amongst whom are Mr. Mappin, the cutler, and his nephew, and Mr. Palmer, son of the celebrated biscuit manufacturer.

At about seven o'clock we entered Christiania Fjord. The rocks at the entrance are very low, one heap being surmounted by a lighthouse. I understand that the navigation of the Fjord is rather intricate, owing to the sunken rocks and islands with which it abounds. We had a glorious sunset, the orb of day disappearing amid a perfect blaze of gorgeous colour at about 9.30 p.m. But although the sun had set we could easily see to read ; indeed, at midnight, tolerably small print was quite distinct. About halfway up the Fjord the hills increased in altitude, and in some places almost met. As we sailed along, in several places we seemed to be completely land-locked, and I couldn't for the life of me make out how we were to proceed ; but still we pressed on, seeming obstacles vanishing as we neared them. Many of the mountains were beautifully shaped, and looked superb in the dim light of eve, with the waves lashing their bases and their lovely garments of pine trees. We passed several picturesque villages, a town, and a lighthouse, very strongly resembling a respectable pig-stye. I had a great wish to remain on deck until we reached our desired haven ; but Mr. Saxon advised us to retire, which we did, Mr. M—— sharing our cabin. I lay awake until the vessel stopped, which was at about 1.30 a.m. Peering through the porthole I had my first view of Christiania.

June 23rd.—We arose early, went on deck, and handed our portmanteaus, &c., to the Custom House officers, who had boarded the "Hero." They passed them ; we gave them to a porter and landed. The city bore a very clean and fresh look, with its various-coloured houses and long streets. We made for the Victoria Hotel, which is a fine building, and had breakfast in a balcony tastefully adorned with shrubs, silvered globes, artificial and real birds, an aquarium, and various other ornate appliances, which overlooked a square decorated in a similar manner and containing a large marquee, from the summit of which floated the banner of Norway. During a capital meal of delicious mullet, pretty birds hopped about the table taking crumbs from us.

Mr. M—— and his nephew having arrived at the hotel, we decided to go with the former to Oscar's Hall, the summer residence of the king. First, however, we called upon Mr. Thomas Bennett, an English gentleman from whom tourists may obtain all information as to travelling in Norway. We changed our money, and rambled in the direction of the palace, a large building with a magnificent approach of fine steps.

We hired a carriage for four, and drove through the West End of the city in the direction of Oscar's Hall. The air was so pure and balmy, the sunshine so bright, and the district so lovely, that what wonder that I should say, in response to Mr. M——'s query as to how I was enjoying myself, "I feel as if I were in Paradise."

The West End consists in a long succession of large and beautiful residences of brilliant colour and tasteful design. Trees waved gracefully on all sides ; laburnams hanging in golden beauty; hawthorn, chestnut, and lilac filling the air with fragrance; and wild flowers interspersing themselves with the trees in varied loveliness. To the left, through openings in the foliage, we caught occasional glimpses of the bay with its steamers, ships, and boats, whilst to the right stretched away a lovely range of hills. The houses we passed were nearly all built of wood, which, being cleverly stuccoed, resembled a beautiful yellow or gray stone very closely.

Oscar's Hall, between which and the town intervened a stretch of richly-wooded country and arable land, is situated on an eminence, and commands an exquisite view of the city. It is a very pretty building, and contains some interesting landscape paintings, also a series of oil paintings representing a Norwegian peasant's life from the cradle to the grave. An agreeable old lady tried to explain them to us as well as she was able, but she couldn't speak English, so we did not benefit much by her kindness. We saw some beautifully carved boxes and bronze statuettes of the Scandinavian kings in several of the rooms, all of which were most tastefully adorned, the chief colours employed in the decoration being dark blue and gold. We ascended a tower, from whence one of the most beautiful scenes I ever witnessed was visible. It is useless my attempting to describe its loveliness. Art could not paint it, neither could orator portray it, or poet successfully laud its glories. Christiania, with its red roofs, its church spires, its shipping, and the tree-covered heights that stretched out on every hand, their bases dipping in the rippling waves, lay beneath us, and I positively revelled in the scene, which must be seen to be understood. We re-entered the carriage and drove back past a large farmhouse, where we noticed a blacksmith busily engaged in shoeing a horse. The clover fields around were almost completely overgrown with dandelion. Mr. Saxon was telling us of a return voyage he made

with a friend from Rotterdam to London some years
ago, and mentioned a circumstance connected with the
landing which impressed me very unfavourably with my
own race. There was a German on board, and on the
stage he was surrounded by roughs, who asked him to
let them carry his portmanteau. He very naturally
refused, as he wished to keep possession. Seeing this
the roughs set on him, pelted him, took his luggage
and threw it into the Thames. Such conduct was dis-
graceful ; and much as I love old England, and proud
as I am of the name of Englishman, I felt utterly dis-
gusted with both as I heard the story. We have much
to learn yet ; and although we are brave and true, &c.,
we are, for the most part, anything but gentlemanly in
our treatment of foreigners. The Norwegians, on being
asked a question by an Englishman in incorrect Norse,
do not grin like baboons, as the English would if a
Norwegian asked them a question in broken English.
They almost invariably treat us with politeness, and I
am most favourably impressed with the race. May my
countrymen, who in spite of their many faults I am
proud of, and at the very name of which, on most
occasions, my heart bounds with admiration, take a
lesson in politeness from their Norwegian neigh-
bours.

We paid our fare and then made for the National
Gallery. We met with a most polite French gentleman,
who chattered incessantly in his native tongue to Mr.
M——. He directed us to a fine building, which he
said was the object of our search, but on entering we
found it to be a museum containing many curiosities.
We likewise mistook the University for the National
Gallery, and, though we walked in several directions,
could not find the right building. The Storthing House,
or House of Parliament, which we passed, is a fine
building.

A terrific and totally unexpected shower overtook us,
so we gave up the search and took refuge beneath an
archway until the tempest had subsided. We then returned to *table d' hôte.* In rambling through the streets
we found that there was little difficulty in translating

the words used to advertise the various articles sold in
the different shops.

Mr. Saxon and Harry went to the National Gallery
after dinner, the true locality of which, with the assist-
ance of a map, they succeeded in discovering. I felt
sleepy, and retired to my chamber.

In the evening we went to the Tivoli, or Cremorne, of
Christiania, as I may call it, with young M——. We
attended a theatre situated within the grounds, and
witnessed the capital performance of a Norwegian drama-
tised version of Jules Verne's celebrated tale, "Round
the World in Eighty Days." The scene in which the
heroine is rescued from death by burning was most
exciting and very pretty, the actress being beautifully
attired and possessing a charming face and figure.

The gardens were rather pleasant, and boasted many
shady retreats ; variegated lamps were displayed in
abundance, and a tolerable band discoursed lively music.
I forgot to mention that at the close of the last scene
but one in the theatre the orchestra struck up the tune
of "God Save the Queen" in fine style. I at first
thought this was in honour of English visitors, but it
seems that the Norwegian national anthem is set to the
same tune as ours.

We met John Smith, the steward of the "Hero,"
and were much amused by the laughable stories he told
us. He is a very nice fellow indeed, and has been
running between various ports on the North Sea for
thirty years. On one occasion he was fourteen days in
crossing from Christiania to Hull. The steamer left so
as to be in time to reach England just before Christmas,
and was laden with game, which persons in Norway
were sending to their friends in England. The weather
was fearful, and, when about half way across the North
Sea, there was a breakage in the machinery. The wind
was very violent, and it was impossible to do anything
except "tack" incessantly. The engines were useless,
and this had to be accomplished by means of what little
canvas could be spread. All the provisions were speedily
demolished, and the game had to be eaten without bread
or seasoning, or vegetables of any kind save three bags

of potatoes belonging to the captain and "John." As may be imagined, this fare was very unpalatable.

At last the rough weather ceased, and with some difficulty the vessel finally managed to reach Hull.

June 24*th.*—After an early breakfast we went to the station and booked for Eidsvold. The carriages are very comfortable, and contain a glass cistern holding water, a tumbler, and cigar-ash boxes. Travellers are requested to deposit the ashes of their cigars in these instead of throwing them through the windows, as forests have frequently been set on fire by non-attendance to this precaution.

The ride was through very pretty though rather tame scenery, similar to much that we see in the picturesque parts of England, save that the houses were of wood, very brightly painted, and the roofs of red tile. Captain Bag, of the steamship " Kong Oscar," plying between Eidsvold and Lilliehammer, rode in the same carriage as we, and was very agreeable.

We embarked with him at Eidsvold on Lake Mjosen. The lake is a regular succession of charming scenes. In some places hills rise in sullen grandeur almost perpendicularly from the shore, their hoary sides brightened, or darkened, if you like the word better, by innumerable pine trees. In others low hills rose gently from the lake—green fields spread out on all sides—lively-looking trees shaded exquisitely pretty houses and white churches, or good-humoured peasants came aboard in small boats. The sky was, save for about half an hour during which the rain came down very heavily, beautifully blue, and the clouds magnificently gilded by the sunbeams, whilst the water was very clear and of a lovely pale green hue. One portion of the lake lay between particularly high and precipitous rocks, and here, we were told by Captain Bag, the water was 240 fathoms deep.

We had a first-rate dinner consisting of salmon— which, when saturated with butter in a liquid state, is positively delicious—roast meat, and lusciously-flavoured blancmange. I can fancy I am eating the latter even now. One of the waitresses was very good-looking, indeed, nicer than any other Norwegian I have seen as yet.

We reached Hamar at 3.30. It is a rather large place, with some extensive and richly-coloured buildings, pleasantly situated on the western shore of the lake. Near it are the ruins of a Roman Catholic cathedral. When the Scandinavians gave up that religion, preferring the doctrines of Luther, they destroyed many of the churches of the old religion and murdered several priests. Hence the present condition of Hamar Cathedral.

Mr. Saxon, at the request of Harry, decided to proceed from Lilliehammer by carriole to-night instead of boarding there as we had intended.

There was a peasant on board selling good knives, something like dirks. As I thought they might come in useful, and would, whether or not, serve as reminiscences of my visit to this lovely land, with which I am every moment becoming more enchanted, I asked him to show me one at two kroner (about 2s. 3d.). He couldn't speak a word of English, and I only knew about twenty words of Norwegian, so we had some difficulty in making ourselves understood.

My last thoughts in connection with the sail on board the " Kong Oscar " were of a lovely Norwegian lass on board. She made me feel just the least bit sentimental, and as a means of showing this I grinned like a monkey. She responded, and then we went ashore, terminating the most enjoyable sail I ever had. Though Captain Bag had telegraphed for carrioles there were none awaiting us at the landing stage, so we entered a barouche and were driven to Fossegarden along the grandest valley I have ever seen as yet. The lake terminates at Lillehammer, where a river tumbles into it from the hills. On each side are majestically sloping mountains clad with most beautiful pines, between which at intervals foam lively little cataracts in their furious efforts to reach the river below which is, I believe, the Logen. Its waters are of a greenish hue. Along its banks runs a good road commanding a fine view of the surrounding eminences and of Lake Mjosen in the

B

distance. Fossegarden is one and a quarter Norsk miles (nine English miles) from Lillehammer. We were expecting to feed on fladbrod there in a miserable kind of hut, and were agreeably surprised to find a most unique and respectable establishment overlooking a noble fall in the river. Snow-white waves with horrent crests go madly plunging over huge rocks with a great and incessant roar, strongly reminding one of frantic white steeds jumping headlong and confusedly downwards.

A woman came to us and, by means of putting our fingers down our throats and making various pantomimic gestures, we made her understand that we were hungry. "Have you any salmon?" asked Mr. Saxon; but she seemed to be "a little bit bothered." "Something to eat!" he exclaimed, for about the sixth time, again putting his fingers down his throat. She shook her head. "Fladbrod!" he shouted in desperation. A gracious smile overspread her countenance, and in ecstacy she replied, "Ya! Ya!" (Yes! Yes!) But, although we had been preparing ourselves for anything and had talked so much about fladbrod, we couldn't help expecting salmon, and felt disappointed. In ten minutes, however, we adjourned to the dining-room and found—what? Well, there was a great plate of fladbrod, which I had better here explain is very similar to oatmeal cake. It is made in the form of a huge fan. But that was not all the provision made for us. There were eggs, two kinds of fish, three kinds of cheese, one of which had a most peculiar flavour as if "a pot of treacle had been upset in it," capital brown bread, delicious Norwegian rusks, good tea and very rich cream; also milk, which had an agreeable taste something like our whey. We were all very jocular at our good luck, and enjoyed the meal immensely. Afterwards, though it still rained heavily, we scrambled down to the fosse (waterfall). Oh! it was a grand sight! Never before had I beheld anything so sublime, and what wonder that my thoughts flew to Him whose praise resounded in every terrific roar?

At 11.15 p.m. we were playing Domino Carte without

either candles or lamps to illumine our chamber, for it was almost as light as day. It was very interesting to observe clouds form on the side of the mountain opposite, gradually ascending higher to mingle or disperse themselves and forming in their course the most wonderful figures. One bore a great resemblance to a fiery dragon, with distended nostrils from which issued a dense smoke, careering frantically along the hills, dragging a huge cloud-chariot in which stood a shadowy, undefinable monster, lashing the steed into fury. Then the figure in the huge vehicle changed into that of a woman whose breast was bared to the heavens and whose arms were lifted in an attitude of supplication.

But it was too late to contemplate the scene longer, so we retired to rest.

June 25*th.*—Breakfasted early and, soon after seven, entered our carrioles, the national vehicles of Norway.

"The carriole somewhat resembles the Italian carricola, and is usually built without springs. The shafts are long and elastic and are fixed to the axle-tree. The seat (which will only hold one person) is placed well forward, and, by cross pieces, rests on the shafts, the elasticity of which serves instead of springs, and prevents the occupant being jolted, except when the roads are very bad. The legs are brought to a nearly horizontal position, and the feet rest in stirrup-shaped irons, so that in descending the steepest hill there is no inconvenience, nor the possibility of being thrown out, in the event of the horse falling. A board is fixed across the ends of the shafts behind the axletree to carry a trunk, and there the boy (or girl, as the case may be) who takes the horse back seats himself. The harness is of the most simple construction, and so contrived as to fit any of the small horses that are met with. There are no traces, and the shafts are attached direct to the substitute for a collar by a peg and loop arrangement, which should be inspected by the traveller at each change. The horses are generally so docile that a child may drive them with perfect safety, if they be not overladen, and the foal may often be seen trotting after the mother by the side of the farmer's carriole. They are matchless for their sureness of foot, in proof of which a broken knee is seldom seen."

We rode up Gudbrandsdalen or "the Gudbrands dale " through several pretty villages, changing horses about every nine miles. Until 2 a.m. it rained very heavily ; but we each had large mackintoshes and umbrellas, whilst the carrioles contained aprons which completely covered us to the waist, so we did not take much harm, though it would have been much pleasanter had the sun shone. The carrioles are by no means uncomfortable and the ponies scarcely need driving. At the first station after Fossegarden we got a car to hold two persons in lieu of two of the carrioles, Harry and I riding with Mr. Saxon in the car alternately, the other taking a carriole. There was much beautiful scenery. During the whole of the journey the river Logen lay at our feet, in many places expanding into moderate sized lakes. On all sides tumbled into it from the mountains picturesque cataracts. The roads were in capital condition. On each side were, for the greater part of the journey, dense forests of the most magnificent trees. Oh! how I longed to transplant some of the young pines into our garden at Bruche, and into what raptures did I fly at the sight of the silvery birches, so gracefully shapen with their delicate branches, rustling, tiny leaves and white and shining barks ! Magpies flew about in all directions, and once or twice we heard the familiar note of the cuckoo. There are none, or scarcely any, singing birds in Norway. Mr. Saxon thought that the magpies and cuckoos, which steal the eggs of smaller birds, were the principal agents in producing this most undesirable state of affairs. We dined at Skjaeggestad, an excellent station, where we fared sumptuously on various totally unexpected delicacies. The hostess was most agreeable. I said to her "Mange tak," which means " many thanks," with the effect of making her still more so. She brought me a large jug containing about a pint and a-half of the richest cream, and some superb milk.

By the time we resumed our journey the rain had

ceased, and it was very pleasant once more to behold
the cheering sunbeams. We got to Listad at about a
quarter to six, passing the octagonal church of Vaenebygden. As it again commenced to rain we decided to
stop here for the night. We were rather astonished
when soon afterwards the Rev. C. E. Brooke and his
wife, whom we had met on board the " Kong Oscar,"
drove up. We had tea, or rather a second dinner, with
them, after which Mr. Saxon retired, as he was rather
unwell, whilst Harry and I inspected Vaenebygden
Church. All the stations so far have been most comfortable, with very tastefully arranged dining and bed-
rooms. At each is kept a " Dag Bog," or Day Book,
in which are inscribed the names of visitors, with the
number of horses they required, and remarks commen-
datory or otherwise. In all the Dag Bogs we have as
yet met with we have found the name of J. C. Phythian,
the talented author of " Scenes of Travel in Norway."
We noticed that most of the window-blinds in Norway
have very pretty pictures printed upon them. The
effect is charming.

June 26th.—Rose early, resolved to travel a long
distance. Passed through Storklevestad, Breden, Moen,
Laurgaard, Bredevangen, Toftemoen, to Dombaas. Beyond Storklevestad we passed a large stone, stating that
Colonel George Sinclair was buried there 26th August,
1612, after the fight of Kringelen, which Laing shall
now describe for us. The scene of the tragedy is where
the road passes a very steep hill. On the spot where
Sinclair fell is a small post.

 " In 1612, during the war between Christian IV. of
Denmark and Gustavus Adolphus of Sweden, a body of
Scotch troops had been raised for the service of Sweden.
The Danes were at that time in possession of Gotten-
burg, and from Calmar in the Baltic to the North Cape
the whole coast was occupied by the subjects of
Christian IV. The Scotch, therefore, decided on the
bold plan of landing in Norway and fighting their way
across it to Sweden. A portion landed at Trondhjem,
and the rest, 900 strong, commanded by Colonel George

Sinclair, landed in Romsdalen, August, 1612, from whence they marched towards this valley. At Kringelen an ambush was prepared by about 300 peasants ; huge quantities of rocks, stones, and trees, were collected on the mountain, and so placed that all could at once be launched upon the road beneath. Everything was done to lull the Scotch into security, and with perfect success. When they arrived beneath the awful avalanche prepared for them, all was sent adrift from above, and the majority of the Scotch were crushed to death, or swept into the river and drowned ; the peasants then rushed down upon the wounded and stragglers, and despatched them. Of the whole force only two of the Scotch are said to have survived. But accounts differ on this point, one being that sixty prisoners were taken, and afterwards slaughtered in cold blood.

"Sinclair's wife is said to have accompanied him ; and, it is added, that a youth who meant to join the peasants in their attack was prevented by a young lady, to whom he was to be married the next day. She, on hearing that one of her own sex was with the Scotch, sent her lover to her protection. Mrs. Sinclair, mistaking his object, shot him dead."

Such is the story, and as we drove along the side of the mountain, I pictured the army marching at its base, the crouching forms of the peasants, their eyes inflamed with hate, the mass of huge stones, the river at the bottom of the hill, the signal, the fall of the avalanche, and the death-wail of the dying.

Just before we reached Moen we passed three splendid cataracts, two of which fell from a height of, I should think, at least a thousand feet, and formed beautiful silver chains on the side of the rugged mountain ; and the other of which burst through an opening in the rocks to our right with tremendous roars, a dense volume of water falling at our feet. We stopped at Moen, entered the house, and were pleased with it. A large grate in one corner of the principal room was filled with branches of a most odorous tree, the floor being strewn with the same. The house was not nearly so elegant as those some of the former stations boast of; but it seemed more Norwegian, and consequently we were pleased with it. Dinner was ordered, and then we were disenchanted. After waiting half an hour, during which we vainly strove to make the skydgaard, or boy who accompanied the carriole, tell us the amount we owed him (for he was most stupid, and elicited from Mr. Saxon the words "th'ar' a nice mon t' turn eawt," to my great amusement), we decided to go on, and bother no more about the dinner. We were putting the pony to the car when an old dame toddled across the yard into the room we had vacated, and laid a table. What a spread! Bad veal, bad beef, bad milk, sour bread, dirty glasses! We didn't eat much. A lazy fellow was lounging about with a pipe in his mouth. After continued asking, he proceeded to yoke our ponies, and after wasting no end of time, we at last left the worst hole I ever visited. From Moen to Laurgaard there was nothing particularly striking except the road, which is in capital condition, and is a wonderful specimen of engineering skill. The old road was just visible most of the way either below or above us. Huge rocks had been riven asunder, deep valleys filled, and fences of gigantic stones, placed about a yard apart, or of wood, constructed along the roadside. The wooden fences in Norway are peculiar. They consist of double upright posts about ten feet in height, tapering off towards the top, connected by layers of slanting poles secured with osiers. Similar fences are ranged across the hay-fields, the hay, owing to the wet climate, being suspended upon them, where it speedily dries. The bridges over the watercourses, many of which are crowded with timber floating down towards the more civilized districts for home use or exportation, are generally very picturesque.

We crossed the Logen at Laurgaard to change our horses, re-crossed it, and drove through a most magnificent pass called Rusten. The mountains draw together, and the stream becomes narrow, rolling with grand reverberations over a bed of terrible rocks. As we drove along the road, to our left, at the foot of awful precipices, foamed the now angry Logen. Across it rose frowning cliffs with dark-looking timber-cloaks, whilst to our right was a lofty tree-covered mountain. We were a tremendous height above the river, which, when almost half way through the pass, we crossed over an interesting wooden bridge. Then there lay before us an eminence much greater than any we had as yet seen, which seemed to frown upon us as we passed. Gradually the pass became wider, and the slope from the road to the river more gentle. We drove through a park-like domain to Toftemoen, where the Gudbrands-dal is ended and the Dovrefjeld begins. It is stated that the station-master here can trace his pedigree to Harold Harfager, and several ancient articles of furni-ture and a genealogical tree are kept in the visitors' room. "Herr Tofte is a rich man, and when King Charles XV. dined at his house on his way to be crowned at Throndhjem in 1860, his uncle, who then kept the station, told His Majesty that it was unneces-sary to bring in his plate, as he had silver forks and spoons enough for all the 30 or 40 in the suite."

Soon after leaving Toftemoen it commenced to rain heavily. I drew the apron of my carriole tightly around me, buttoned my mackintosh, and prepared to face the bad weather, for, according to Mr. Saxon, we had yet to go fourteen English miles. I had had quite enough carriole driving for one day. I was very cold and had sprained my wrist; and I grumbled to myself very furiously about the foolishness of going at such a pace, for we had already travelled forty-four miles since break-fast. But grumbling was of no avail, as Mr. Saxon had resolved to continue the journey (and I afterwards found that he was quite right in so doing).

We gradually left the rocky district through which we had hitherto travelled and ascended a very steep sandy hill. Hundreds of feet below us was the Logen. Higher and higher we went until we had almost attained the summit of the loftiest elevation we had as yet sighted. On, on through the rain and cold—on, on towards Dombaas. What a time we seemed in reaching it! It was but seven miles from Toftemoen, but the miles seemed leagues. And then the thought came that we should, even at the termination of the present drive, have another of seven miles. I almost, at the time, wished I'd never seen Norway. At last we saw a large building which the Skydgaard said was our destination, and never was I more delighted than with the news. We reached it, got out, and found that three French gentlemen, whose acquaintance we had made at Listad, and who had kept ahead of us during the day, intended staying here all night, and had very kindly ordered for us dinner and apartments, so Mr. Saxon decided to stop. This was glorious news. We found a large fire burning in a stove in the dining-room and soon congregated around it chattering gaily in French, Norwegian and English, though I must say that *our* efforts at the two former were rather ludicrous. Dombaas is a telegraph station. From it the road branches off along the Dovrefjeld Mountains to Trondhjem. It is situated at a great elevation. Reindeer, bears and wolves roam over the surrounding mountains, as a proof of which I may say that we had reindeer steak, about the most delicious dish I ever tasted, for supper, or dinner, which word would better describe the excellent spread of which we partook. In the hall were suspended some beautiful skins of Arctic wolves, snow-white and remarkably soft, of bears and of foxes.

June 27th.—Left Dombaas at an early hour in company with the Frenchmen, who are most polite, agreeable and amusing. From various things we noticed we thought they must be the contractors for the line of telegraph which runs from Christiania to Molde.

The scenery we had hitherto passed through was, according to the Guide Book, only pretty, and now we were coming to the grandest part of Norway, *i.e.*, the Romsdal.

We dined at Lesje Jernvaerk. We were much interested in the contemplation of the dwelling-room of the house. On one side of the window hung a pair of spectacles and a long Norwegian pipe. On the sill were a Bible and Prayer-book, whilst suspended to the other side was another pair of spectacles. What a tale it told of the long, dreary winter days, when for month after month the ground was thickly covered with snow, which rendered outdoor exercise almost impossible for the old couple. In fancy, we saw the man sitting by the fire puffing slowly away at the pipe—his wife, with the Bible in her hands, reading aloud to him of that land where there shall be no sorrow, nor age, nor long and dreary winter, but perpetual joy and youth and glorious summer. We could imagine the tears trickling down the furrowed countenances as they read of the sufferings of their great Master, and the joy which would beam in their eyes as they searched the precious promises of lasting guidance and an abundant entrance into the eternal kingdom. It was, indeed, very touching.

Here we examined a saw-mill. I cannot stop to describe the Norwegian mills; but they are capitally arranged, being turned by water, which is here so plentiful.

At Stueflaaten, the next station, we noticed several English novels, including "The Antiquary," by Sir Walter Scott, and "The Caxtons," by Lord Lytton. I may here just mention that the Norwegians do not keep their photographs in albums as we do; but have them all framed and hung up in the principal room of the house. We noticed this at almost every station.

Along the road we were continually passing cows, calves, sheep, goats, and pigs. The calves, which were remarkably graceful animals, were terrified at the sound of our carrioles, and almost invariably ran from us in deepest alarm. The pigs were a combination of dirty yellow, black, and red in colour, and were most de-testable-looking creatures.

Soon after leaving Stueflaaten, where we first saw the river Rauma, having at last lost sight of the Logen, we dismounted to look at a beautiful double fall in the river. Exquisite violets grew upon its brink. I never before saw such magnificent wild - flowers as those we passed from Lilliehammer to this place. Great banks absolutely covered with gorgeous masses of pink, white, yellow, or blue blossom were scattered in profusion along our path; and their sweet odour and delightful appearance added very greatly to the pleasure of our tour. But I am digressing.

We were driving along the brink of a precipice, the bottom of which was invisible, when the Frenchmen stopped and got out. We did not know what this was for, but we imitated their example. We did not notice a board on which was painted the word Stettefos, and that a footpath led to a wooden bridge over the river. Ah! it must be a waterfall!

It was, and such a one as I never saw before! Such a grand and totally unexpected scene burst upon us as we reached the bridge that my breath was fairly taken away, and every sense was wrapped in silent contemplation.

Tumbling down over a great wall of rock, which ran across the ravine between the great high sides of which flowed the river, was a mass of seething, boiling, bubbling, hissing water. Down into a terrible depth at our feet it roared, making the bridge tremble as if in direst fear. Lovely green was the primary colour of this liquid mass ; but as it rebounded from rock to rock it was lashed into such a fury that a great angry torrent of purest foam sprang from the green and shrouded it in glistening whiteness. The rocks around rose in awful grandeur; and we shuddered as we thought of the possibility of a fall into the yawning abyss.

Every hill was tipped with light, and the great foaming waves that rolled over the jagged rocks flashed with the golden sunbeams. Around us grew the most delicate ferns, and before us towered mountains whose summits were white with the lingering snows of winter. What grandeur, what sublimity was before us! Mundane thoughts in me gave place to thoughts celestial. The roar of the cataract reverberated with the voice of Him who is mightier than the noise of many waters. The glistening of the sunbeams on the distant snow-capped mountains seemed to be His smile. The canopy of light above us was but the roof of His glorious pavilion, and the ferns were a proof of His bounteous love.

We lingered long at this superb spot, and turned reluctantly away to pursue our course. The road went

lower and lower and now led into the world-famed
valley, the Romsdal. Oh! as I come to describe its
loveliness, how I feel my own utter insignificance. I
used to think I knew something, but I am now un-
deceived. My descriptive powers seem as weak in
comparison to the exquisiteness of the scene as a drop
of water is small when compared to the ocean. I feel
awed, confounded, an earth-worm, an atom, yea, a very
nothing. It seems almost like presumption on my part
to attempt a description. Byron, that grand genius,
with all the might of his poetic soul, would be utterly
unequal to the task. The most eminent artist would
find himself at fault if he tried to portray the Romsdal.
It needs the Maker of these mighty mountains and
valleys and rocks and trees to tell of their beauty.
Cherubim and seraphim cannot proclaim the majesty of
these great works, but point to the greater Creator.
How, then, shall my poor stammering tongue serve to
tell you of the Romsdal, one of nature's masterpieces?
But I'll do my best.

Suddenly rounding a huge rock we found ourselves on the
brink of a river, flowing through a narrow plain bounded
by two chains of insurmountable and snow-crowned
cliffs. On all sides seemed to fall from the heavens great
streaks of water with an incessant thunder. Down they
leaped, almost perpendicularly, whipped into whiteness
in their mad career, and falling amid a dense smoke
among boulders themselves almost as large as mountains, through which, in bubbling streams, they ran to
join the rapid-flowing river. Most of the falls seemed
composed of an endless succession of snow storms, each
storm culminating in a deliciously-curved wreath, and
each wreath again disuniting to repeat the operation.
The cliffs, almost desolate, were gilded gloriously by
the sunbeams which burst over their summits, and the
snow which crowned them seemed to connect itself im-
perceptibly with the gorgeous clouds that floated in a
sky of the deepest azure. Some of the falls were almost
lost in spray owing to the tremendous height from which
they descended. At one point, just ahead of us, on a
sloping mountain was a great snow patch which bore a

most striking resemblance to Napoleon Bonaparte upon a milk-white charger galloping over the hills. Then came another remarkable fall. A great stream of water poured tolerably smoothly down an undulating portion of a very high mountain. Suddenly it reached a huge precipice whose summit overhung the base. Over this it leaped in nine snake-like coils, which twined and twisted and hissed in the most beautiful manner imaginable, finally shooting amid a chaotic mass of granite, losing itself for a time, and then flowing peacefully amid silvery birches to the river.

At Ormen there had lately been an awful avalanche. We could easily trace its course, for a portion of a great forest had been uprooted, and where once was luxuriant vegetation was now scantily covered with grass. The innumerable fosses or falls we were passing began gradually to lessen in quantity, and the valley widened a little. The mountains became yet more perpendicular, and, on turning a corner, the sun, which had hitherto been concealed, burst upon us with more than wonted magnificence. The boulders became less and less frequent, and verdant grass spread out to our right and left from which sprang the most shapely birches. If we looked behind us we saw frowning rocks; if before us, frowning rocks; to the right, frowning rocks; to the left, frowning rocks. We seemed completely hemmed in. Overhead was the loveliest sky I had ever seen, with amber-coloured flashing clouds peering over the cliffs and floating in a sky of delicious ether. It was easy to imagine that we were in a vast cathedral, the firmament for its nobly decorated roof, the grass its beautiful floor, and the eternal hills its grandific walls. And whether it were a cathedral or no I there heard such a sermon as never proceeded from the lips of the most eloquent divine. In ten thousand tones of softest music, and twice ten thousand roars of splendour, was God eulogised and atheism denounced. The hills, the heavens, the fosses, the trees, the river—all were discoursing on the goodness of the Omnipotent, and my heart was stirred to its innermost depths by Nature's sublime oration.

Wilder and wilder grew the scene. The smooth summits of the huge walls around us were now riven into hundreds of fantastic forms. Churches with "storied windows richly dight," through which streamed rays of heavenly lustre, spires towering upwards, gable-ends of ruined houses, lions couchant and rampant, obelisks, domes, minarets, cones and impregnable walls surrounding frowning castles—all seemed " cut into the sky."

Mile after mile we rode onwards, our interest never halting for a second, but, on the contrary, receiving fresh stimulus every moment. It was one panorama of grandeur indescribable, and we positively revelled in glories such as hitherto our eyes had never seen, our wildest imaginings never conceived. It was after ten o'clock and the sun was only then just disappearing over the loftiest elevation, throwing out radii in all directions.

At last we sighted the Romsdal Horn, which was conspicuous above all the surrounding eminences. I can best describe it as a huge cone from the side of which springs a smaller cone. It is perfectly awe-inspiring in its bare and rugged loneliness, and we shuddered at the very contemplation of it. It was for a long time deemed insurmountable, but a blacksmith recently succeeded in scaling its terrible walls and planting in triumph a flag upon its summit.

Towards eleven o'clock we drew up opposite the Hotel Aak, and even then the sun had not sunk below the horizon, for his rich beams, of a kind of crimson-amber hue, flooded the Horn with celestial radiance. The valley widened out a little, and the hotel was situated on a gentle slope leading down through fertile fields and graceful trees to the river. The hotel, which, by the way, is simply a good-sized house, not in the least resembling an hotel in our acceptance of the word, as are most of the country so-called hotels, was most comfortable. There was a book kept in which many visitors, most of whom stayed for a long time fishing, &c., expressed their admiration of the situation, the kindness of the host and his daughters, the excellence of the fare, and the enjoyment they had experienced in visiting the splendid district. There were several counts, lords, baronets, and eminent personages in the list. Aak was the summer quarters of Lady di Beauclerc during her residence in "the land of the midnight sun," which she has celebrated in a delightful work, "A Summer and Winter in Norway." We were quite as pleased as our predecessors, and after a most excellent supper retired to rest at quarter past twelve, it being as light as it generally is in England at seven o'clock at this time of the year.

June 28th.—Before breakfast Mr. Saxon, Harry, and the *très-jolis* Frenchmen took a stroll towards the river ; but I was unable to go as I wished to write my journal. When they returned one of the Frenchmen bore a prettily-marked snake upon a long stick. It seems that as they strolled onwards they were suddenly startled by a wriggling object springing up in their path, which they mistook for an eel. But it spat angrily at them, and then they discovered their mistake. A Frenchman raised his stick and caught it a heavy whack, with the effect of stunning it, and having killed it, they fastened it to the stick and brought it to the hotel as a trophy.

After breakfast we walked slowly to Veblungnaes on the Fjord. It is a rather interesting village. I was much struck by our passing several houses with the doors locked and the keys either left in the locks or hung outside upon the wall. What a tale this told of Norwegian honesty, and how different is this to what we see in England ! If keys were left in doors of un-protected residences in our country, I fancy the doors would soon be opened by persons other than the owners, and that the money, furniture, and everything else of value would speedily vanish. Ah ! although we boast of being the greatest nation in the world, we have much to learn, even from Norway.

At 2.30 p.m. we embarked on the "Molde," a small steamer which sailed down the Fjord to Molde. The scenery was very pretty. At one part of the voyage we

were struck by seeing an enormous mountain against
the bare summit of which dark clouds charged furiously.
Near this spot we were much interested in watching the
motions of a large fish which every few seconds rose to
the surface, swam for a few yards, and disappeared.
We could not make out what it was; but thought it
resembled a whale in shape. Later on in the day we
learnt from a gentleman on the " Haakon Jarl " that a
whale fifteen yards long had been seen that morning to
enter the Fjord by the inhabitants of Molde. We passed
several " breeding islands," upon which clustered eider
ducks, and scores of other sea-fowl.

Molde, where we arrived at about seven o'clock, is a
very pretty little town built at the foot of a picturesque
hill. We spent ten minutes in perambulating the
principal streets. Our luggage was then transferred to
the " Haakon Jarl," and we were taken on board in a
small boat. It is a new vessel, and I never saw one
more easy in its motion or more complete in its construction. On board we found a most polite, agreeable,
and intelligent gentleman, who resides in Norway eleven
months out of the twelve. He is of Danish descent,
was born in England, travels for a large Birmingham
firm, and he told us that his name was L. B. Grondhind.
Although he has been in Norway for several years, and
has gone almost all over it by carriole, sledge, car, and
steamer, he has never yet met with a snake in the
country. This struck us as very peculiar, and made us
esteem our capture even more than we had hitherto
done.

We had originally intended to go to Aalesund, and
from thence down the Sogne and Hardanger Fjords,
finally sailing from Bergen. But our French acquain-
tances were very eager in persuading us to go to
Bergen at once, as there was, according to them,
nothing worth seeing at Aalesund. This involved a
little difficulty at first, as we had quite made up our
minds to go to the latter; but our Birmingham friend
confirmed them in their statement as to the superiority
of Bergen, and we came to the resolution to go there
and inspect the Fjords from thence. At about eleven

we stopped at Aalesund, which is prettily situated between two hills.

June 29th.—All day we were steaming away up the countless creeks and among the rocky islets which abound on this most indented coast. The scenery was very pretty, particularly in the neighbourhood of one or two villages where we stopped to receive large boxes of herrings, which were brought to the ship in boats.

Mr. Saxon was full of lively anecdote, and contributed much to the enjoyment of the sail. As we stood gazing at the rocks he told us the following :—

"An Irish pilot was sent on board a vessel to conduct it along a dangerous coast. The captain, after some time had elapsed, began to mistrust him. 'Do you know all the rocks about here?' he asked. Just then the ship struck with a terrific crash upon a concealed mass of granite. 'Bedad and I do, and that's one of thim !' was the reply."

I quote the above as a sample of Mr. Saxon's jovial disposition, and as one of the laughable stories of which he seems to possess an inexhaustible store.

At 7.45 p.m. we were steaming slowly up the bay at the head of which stands Bergen.

We landed and drove to Holdt's Hotel, where we had dinner, afterwards going for a stroll. It was Sunday, and all the people were dressed in their best. Sunday is a grand day in Norway, for after 4 o'clock dancing and other pastimes are engaged in with vehemence. However, I am not quite correct in calling this lively time Sunday. The real Norwegian Lord's day commences, if I am rightly informed, at 4 p.m. on our Saturday, and terminates at 4 p.m. the next day. The religion is Lutheran and, on the whole, the people are very devout—infinitely more so than the English, I am sorry to say.

Bergen is a very picturesque city. It was founded in 1070 A.D. by King Olaf Kyrre, who made it the second city in his dominions. Shortly afterwards, owing to its advantageous situation, and the privileges granted to merchants of the Hanseatic League, several of whom

had settled there and erected a factory, it became the
first city.   It retained its place until within the last few
years, and has, even now, more trade than Christiania.
The present population is, I believe, about 45,000.   It
is the scene of several remarkable events, which I
cannot here enter into.   It has several times suffered
dreadfully from fire, being, like other Norwegian towns,
timber-built.   In 1488 eleven churches, and the greater
part of the town were destroyed ; and in 1855, one
hundred and eighty houses were burnt in the west part
of the city.   Nothing could have saved the rest but for
the broad market-place, beyond which the flames were
prevented from spreading.

Bergen supplies almost the whole of the South of
Europe with fish, and has a very great fish-market.   It
contains some fine and interesting buildings, including
the Fortress of Bergenhuus, St. Mariae-kirke, which
Snorro says existed in the year 1181, the Cathedral, the
Gallery of the Art Union, Museum, and Arbeider-
Forening or Workmen's Club.   There is a hospital for
lepers here, the disease being by no means rare on the
coast of Norway.

June 30th.—After a most refreshing bath and a
capital breakfast I strolled through the city, intent on
climbing a mountain which rose beyond the castle, and
which, according to Mr. G——, commanded a splendid
view.   Mr. Saxon and Harry were too—well, I won't say
what ; but they didn't care for climbing, so they
rambled about the city instead.

Having passed a bronze statue of Christie, situated in
one of the finest streets, I walked past the Market Hall,
a handsome building, and commenced the ascent.   I
was told that the mountain was only 1,800 feet high, and
I imagined it an easy matter to reach the summit.   Not
so easy as I thought, though, for I toiled slowly and
painfully up, the perspiration pouring from me, it being
very hot.   (By the way, I must here tell you that rain
falls in Bergen 200 days out of the 365 in a year.)

When, however, I reached the summit, near which
stands a huge weathercock, I felt amply repaid for my

trouble, for a glorious panorama lay before me. Just at my feet was the city itself. The most thickly inhabited portion is situated on a tongue of land which runs far out into the bay. On each side, separated from the tongue by lovely inlets one of which is thickly studded with steamers, ships and boats, were more houses, built at the foot of two mountains, on one of which I sat. I saw the cleanly streets with "the busy tide of flesh and blood," carts, carrioles and cars rolling along them and looking like mites in the distance. I saw a sea of red roofs with here and there a skylight gleaming in the sunbeams, and at intervals, towering above it like lighthouses, were visible lofty spires. Verdant lawns were profusely scattered around and luxuriant trees lent brightness to the scene. Eastward, a pretty valley ran into the mountains, in which were embosomed several picturesque lakes bordered by large patches of timber, gardens and fields, and farther still, to the very edge of the horizon, rose peak after peak in misty splendour. Seawards stretched rocks innumerable intersected in all directions by the waters of the ocean, which were now as "calm as a bowl of milk." Behind me were fierce black clouds which rumbled furiously as a gentle breeze wafted them northwards, whilst within a few yards strolled nimble sheep, the bells which are suspended around their necks tinkling pleasantly as they moved. It was, indeed, a lovely view, and long did I linger to contemplate its beauties. I placed a stone upon a cairn built at one of the highest points and commenced to descend. The mountain was very steep in some parts and I was in imminent peril of breaking my neck ; but before me sparkled a fosse and I was resolved to go down along its brink. Over a boggy watercourse I leaped and at last stood near the place where, with a roar, a liquid mass went splashing and fuming down to the sea. When I reached the foot of the hill I found that I was in a part of Bergen some distance from Holdt's Hotel. Past an old two-towered church I sauntered, down to the quay, where lay a host of vessels of all shapes and sizes and upon the borders of which were built dozens of long warehouses. Then

I lost my way and was rambling round Christie's statue and the neighbourhood for about half-an-hour. It was fearfully hot and I was fearfully tired; and I couldn't help exclaiming, "hang it!" "dash it!" "confound it!" &c. This did not do a bit of good, though, and hindered rather than accelerated my movements. Getting into a temper is very foolish. Keep cool, and difficulties are easily surmounted. I know a person who, if he cannot open a door at the first attempt, kicks it most frantically; but the door takes no heed and his boots get worn out the sooner for his trouble.

At last I managed to sight the desired haven and, with a sigh of relief, sank upon a comfortable couch therein, regaling myself with lemonade and pastry.

Mr. Saxon, Harry and the Frenchmen had visited the Museum and other places of interest in the city during my ramble on the mountain.

After dinner at six, Harry and I went to witness a dramatical performance at the Bergen Theatre. The place was crowded, as it deserved to be, for the acting and singing were superb, whilst the actress was simply lovely.

July 1st.—Rose very early and in company with the Frenchmen, whose names are M. Josef Sissener, inspector of telegraphs in Norway, M. Aubron, a Parisian solicitor, and M. Droin, a French journalist, went on board "Hardangeren," that is "The Hardanger," steamship. "En" is the definite article, or distinguishing adjective, if you like, in Norwegian. We were bound for the Hardanger Fjord. A very nice English gentleman sailed with us, who has lived at Bergen for some time. I had a long talk with him about Norway, Sweden and Denmark.

There was a large number of peasants on board, who, to while away the time and vary the monotony of a sea voyage, sang some of their favourite airs very sweetly. Oh! the charms of music! Timid, shrinking hearts it fires with bravery! Mourning, sorrowful spirits it thrills with heavenly ecstacy! Natures hard and harsh its gentle cadences can melt into fountains of purity and gentleness ! Smiles can it scatter where whilom melancholy roamed ! Giddiness and sin can it subdue and into despicable men pour the germs of true nobility ! How its whisperings harmonise with the peace which all at times experience and which passeth understanding ; and how well does it celebrate our triumphs over the powers of darkness ! Music, delightful music ! May thine be not merely the poor perishable wreath with which I strive to deck thee ; but a crown which fadeth not away !

Many of the peasants were dressed very peculiarly. I find myself at a loss to describe their attire. The majority of the females wore great loose black caps, very much like clumsily made bags, ornamented round the edges. They had black jackets and short dresses, which in many instances revealed red stockings. Others had great white calico affairs, somewhat resembling candle extinguishers, upon their heads; and some wore a dress with a red bodice and green sleeves. They looked very picturesque. As for the men, they dress very similarly to the English, and so, indeed, do many of the women. Both are almost invariably good-natured, polite, obliging and honest. The expression of their faces is remarkably English, of which race they are exceedingly fond.

The scenery through which we passed was very pretty. At times we rode upon large sheets of water bounded by low and barren hills, with gentle waves coursing slowly around us. A few minutes more and we found ourselves in narrow channels, no wider than small rivers, with rocks rising on all hands covered with a mass of foliage from summit to base, whilst the water, almost like glass, laved their stony shores. Here and there a group of pretty houses lay before us embowered in vegetation. At many of these groups we stopped to await the arrival of small boats, which brought off passengers.

In the afternoon we caught sight of the Folge Fond Glacier, which is over forty miles in length, and passed several pretty waterfalls ; also a large island, where a most agreeable gentleman who had travelled with us went ashore. There was an iron mine on it, of which he was manager. His wife and daughters were going to England on the same boat as we ; so he entrusted them to our care.

At another place we saw, great ravages had recently been committed by a bear. It had eaten a large number of sheep, and, notwithstanding the efforts of forty or fifty farmers who had armed themselves and gone in pursuit, had not then been captured.

Towards midnight a great wind arose. How the waves would have risen had we been out on the ocean ! But we were almost land-locked, and consequently the sea was tolerably smooth. Nevertheless, the awning was almost riven from the vessel, and like a demon the blast howled round the masts, down the hatchways, and amid the rigging. Fierce black clouds scowled across the lowering sky, and a dreadful twilight fell upon us, through which loomed great, jagged, barren cliffs whose heads were swathed in sepulchral whiteness. We seemed to be in the infernal regions—cut off from humanity—and sailing in a phantom ship over a river of death. We almost shuddered as we contemplated the endless bleakness of the surrounding eminences, and were in momentary expectation of seeing a dreadful fiery spirit appear upon the summit of a desolate crag and thunder forth direst anathemas over our devoted heads, or the misty shadow of some departed Viking with death-like quiet glide along the terrible steeps.

We had been travelling since six in the morning and were utterly wearied, so we entered the smoke-room and sought repose. At 1 a.m. we were aroused by an echoing blast from the steam-horn aboard " Hardangeren," which announced our proximity to Odde, our destination. Here we were conducted to comfortable quarters. I was told a murder had been committed in our bed-chamber, but, in the first place, I didn't believe it, and in the second, even if I had, it wouldn't have made any difference, so I hopped into bed and sank into a deep slumber.

July 2nd.—We awoke late, having slept famously. About the first words I remember being spoken were by Mr. Saxon, and to the effect that M. S—— had just gone down stairs in his night-shirt to give his orders as to breakfast.

It rained heavily until towards eleven o'clock, so of course we were unable to go out. We spent the time in watching two old Norwegian females making fladbrod. One took a handful of dough, made a small cake of it and passed it to the other, who rolled it out until it had become rather large. She then returned it. It was rolled yet more, and finally, having attained a circumference of about three yards, was sprinkled with flour and deposited upon an iron shelf placed over a wood fire. It was soon sufficiently done, when one of the women rolled it up in the form of a huge fan and laid it on a table containing a heap of others. We were invited to taste, and did, to our mutual satisfaction.

The weather at last clearing up, we set out for the Buerbrae Glacier, a part of the Folge Fond, accompanied by the brother of our hostess, who is most obliging and speaks English well. After an enjoyable row over the Sandven Vand, or Lake, during which we unwound a long reel for fishing with the object of entangling some member of the finny tribe, though we were unsuccessful, we landed at a small village and set off up a valley through which foamed a torrent of snow-coloured water. The scenery was very pretty, great mountains arising on both sides covered with trees, and the view before us being terminated by an exquisitely-tinted glacier. The path in some parts was rather steep, but it was ever near the brink of the stream, which frequently fell in a series of foaming cascades, and was ever surrounded by loveliness, both animal, vegetable, and mineral.

Distance is very deceptive in mountainous countries. We had hitherto had abundant proof of this, but the walk we were now taking demonstrated it yet more plainly. From the lake we imagined we could reach the glacier easily in twenty minutes, whereas it took us fully two hours. We were rather wearied when at last we stood at the foot of the Buerbrae, but its glories amply compensated for the fatigue we experienced. " Trials make triumphs all the greater," says S. Holland in one of her capital tales, and she is quite right.

A great block of snow, frozen into the consistency of ice, stretched across the valley. It was broken into every conceivable shape, and huge blocks hung loosely in all parts, which at any moment might have been precipitated upon us. White was the principal colour, but intermingled with it and adding tenfold to its beauty were large patches of many-shaded blue. The sunlight streaming upon it tipt it with brilliancy and lit up the surrounding hills and trees and flowers, of which there were innumerable quantities, with celestial radiance.

The glacier is the nearest to the sea of any in Norway, and is advancing very rapidly down the valley, to the injury of a farm built a little below it. In 1870 the Buerbrae advanced ninety yards, and four yards during one week in 1871. To stand at the lower end is unsafe, as blocks of ice and stone are continually falling.

By the time we reached the lake again the wind had risen greatly, and it required all the strength of our guide to hold the boat with any degree of steadiness whilst we got in and sat down. However, this was at last accomplished, he followed us and pushed off from the shore. The waves were very high and the boat tossed about tremendously. The guide exerted all his strength, but could only just manage to cope with the billows. We made slow progress, and the water kept pouring over the gunwale until there was a regular pool beneath our feet, whilst M. A—— and Harry were saturated. We were in constant danger of being swamped, and a stern expression came over the face of even the boatman. At this terrible moment we chanced to look up and there hanging midway between earth and heaven at the distance of half a mile, apparently, were two uncouth-looking black objects. They were motionless and seemed to frown darkly upon us. With awe-struck voices we asked each other the meaning of the strange sight. Coming as they did in the midst of our danger and perplexity they might easily have been

construed into ghastly portenders of evil, and to a
superstitious mind they certainly looked very like the
supernatural. As for me, I could make them into
nothing reasonable save some strange phenomena of
nature ; and it was not without a certain dread that I
gazed fixedly towards them. The waves, meanwhile,
were constantly increasing in volume, and it was with
the greatest difficulty that the boat made headway.
Now we came to the spot where the torrent poured into
the lake, creating a perfect tumult of waters. Quiet as
death we sat, and the guide pulled with all his might.
The water poured upon us, and we thought it was all
up! I began to calculate as to how far I was able to
swim, and wondered if our French friends could keep
themselves afloat, and whether, in case they could not,
I should be able to support any of them to shore. Any-
how, I resolved to try. As for Mr. Saxon and Harry, I
had been informed that they both understood the art of
propulsion of the body through water. I would advise
all my readers to learn to swim at once, for it is one of
the pleasantest, the most invigorating, and the most
useful athletic exercises in existence, and may some
day stand them in good stead.

Fortunately we did not need to test our powers on
this occasion, for the guide by his wondrous presence of
mind, strength, and skill urged our not very well-con-
structed craft past the most dangerous part of the lake
in safety ; and in process of time we shot between two
huge rocks, sprang from the boat, and stood ashore
again, with gratitude in our hearts to Him who had
delivered us from terrible peril by water.

As we descended the hill up which we had climbed to
the lake, we noticed a long wire running from the
summit of a lofty mountain to our left above our heads,
and finally, as we thought, sinking into the earth to our
right. Upon it were suspended two dark objects, which
we presumed were the same as those which had scared
us on the lake. It seemed to me to be a telegraph wire,
but deeming my opinion on the subject insufficient. I
said to Mr. Saxon, "What's that wire for ?" "It's for
howd th' mountain up!" was his most amusing response.

We had a first-rate dinner at seven, two ladies from Bergen, Fröken (Miss) Lina Olsen and Fröken Hanne Olsen, who have been staying here a fortnight, dining with us. I amused M. S—— immensely by the heartiness of my appetite. He kept passing me plate after plate and dish after dish of delicacies, supposing " Monsieur Bennett," as he called me, to have the digestive powers of a Gargantua, I should think.

July 3rd.—To our extreme regret we parted with the Frenchmen, who went on towards Christiania. They are three of the nicest gentlemen I ever met, and M. Josef S—— is a most amusing old fellow. I shall not speedily forget their kindness, neither will the episode of his going to order breakfast in his night-dress readily sink into oblivion.

At twelve o'clock we started in two cars for the Laathefos, accompanied by our guide of yesterday. We had a most enjoyable drive along the brink of Lake Sandven and on through a superb valley, down which tumbled a river. We passed many noble falls and at last reached our destination. In addition to the Laathefos there roars by its side the Skarfos and, across the stream, the Espelandfos. Of the sister fosses the one's greatest grandeur is where the water leaps over the ridge of a high cliff, and falls almost perpendicularly for about two-thirds of the distance to the river, when its descent becomes more gradual and less interesting ; whilst the other is comparatively tame in its bound from the summit, attaining its terror-inspiring appearance after about a third of its fall, when it dives over a precipitous ledge amid a heap of rocks with the roar of hundreds of cannon, and, uniting with the other, side by side they rush beneath a quaint stone bridge to join the torrent which flows to the lake. Great showers of spray, dense as smoke, rise from the rocks and ascend towards the azure heavens, falling upon the adjacent road with a continuous downpour. Flowers of heavenly hue flourish on the surrounding hills, and a few yards higher up the road the Espelandfos, in a mass of shimmering whiteness, bounds down a precipice, and mingles its waters with the stream.

July 4th.— Having learnt from Fröken Aga (our hostess and daughter of the proprietor of the hotel), that the mysterious wire we had noticed on Wednesday, and which Mr. Saxon said was "for howd th' mountain up," was really intended to lower wood from the high slopes, and that the dark objects which had dumbfounded us whilst on the lake were bundles of faggots secured to the wire, we took a walk in that direction for the purpose of inspecting it more minutely. A pretty little dog from the hotel accompanied us. The bundles of wood we had previously noticed had disappeared, thus confirming Fröken Aga's explanation. The wire, which at first had seemed to run into the earth, we now found was secured to a wooden roller by turning which it could be tightened. The upper end was fastened to a tripod on the mountain side. I lightly touched the wire and it commenced to vibrate most frantically, every second increasing its motion, which continued for a very long time. Thus, it was only necessary to attach the wood hewn on the mountain side, to just touch the wire, and the vibrations would have the effect of hurrying the bundles towards the valley for the use of the peasants.

As I marvelled at the wonderful effect a gentle shake of the wire had upon it, I could not help pondering over the proverb, "Behold how great a fire a small spark kindleth," and its deep significance. The small aperture through which a drop of water trickles into the hold of a vessel, may result in that vessel's awful foundering! "A bow drawn at a venture" may occasion the destruction of the most degraded villain that ever breathed! The first wrong step may lead to a wasted life, a demoniacal death! A word spoken in season may heal a bruised spirit, comfort a broken heart, illumine a dark pathway, and make an erring one turn from the error of his ways to a career of uprightness, nobility, and heavenly-mindedness! Don't despise little things, for

"The massive gate of circumstance
Is turned upon the smallest hinge."

At half-past one, after partaking of the wine and cake so kindly proffered by Fröken Aga, and writing our names in the Dagbog, where I found several signatures of lords, baronets, and other eminent personages, including Thomas Brassey, Esq., M.P., and his wife, who had sailed hither in the "Sunbeam," we embarked again on "Hardangeren," bound for Eide. It was most amusing to see the crowd which had assembled on the quay, if I may so call it, to witness the arrival and departure of the steamship. All the village seemed to have turned out, and one would have imagined it to have been the only sight they had ever witnessed. They manifested as much eagerness as a heap of little boys do in England to hear the lively strains of a brass band. A number of fine cows and several large sacks of flour were unloaded here. The two Olsens accompanied us.

Of all the places we have yet visited I like Odde the best. Perhaps some of you will think this rather odd, but it is a fact, nevertheless. The place is so homely, the people so kind, and the surrounding scenery so grand, that I felt quite reluctant to leave it ; and amongst the many pleasant faces that linger in my memory in connection with Norway will ever stand prominent that of our kind-hearted hostess, Fröken Aga.

The captain and first mate of "Hardangeren" speak English pretty well and are very agreeable. There was a poor madman on board who, under the charge of two men who never left him for a moment, was being taken to an asylum at Bergen. I learnt from the mate that he had only been in this pitiable condition for eight days. Our passage was both speedy and enjoyable ; and soon after five o'clock we landed at Eide, to be greeted by my kind English friend of Tuesday last, who had left us at Eide. We could only obtain one car for the three of us and the skydgaard ; but we had resolved to reach Vossevangen that night, and, in spite of obstacles, must set out. The skyd sat between the legs of Mr. Saxon and Harry, who were on the seat, which just holds two, whilst I perched on our travelling requisites and a sack of hay, to my extreme discomfort.

The scenery was very pretty; indeed, I think for pictu-resque effect it excelled any we have seen. It was very sad that I must perforce gaze upon it whilst in such misery. I got almost crazy at last, so Harry changed places with me. This was, to me, a blessed arrangement, and I thanked him heartily. He himself seemed rather to desire the change ; but Mr. Saxon, wishing to prove the fallacy of his ideas as to the comfort of the back seat, told me not to take the slightest notice if he spoke. This he speedily did—in fact, he poured a volley of questions and remarks into our ears ; but we never vouchsafed a reply. The jolting began to take effect also, and when at last we sighted a place where I could obtain a carriole, I fancy he was by no means sorry.

Perhaps I had better here just mention that the cars are like old and clumsy sand carts with a chair for two hooked upon them, leaving space behind for bags, parcels and the skyd. If we presented a skyd with a gratuity he invariably shook hands with us. Mr. Saxon thought that this action was intended to convey the idea that the recipient had not lost his dignity by ac-cepting the gift. This practice of handshaking pre-vails not only among the skyds, but amongst the Nor-wegian peasants generally, who are extremely polite and nearly always raise their hats on meeting with travellers, whom they expect to respond.

Our route, after traversing the shores of a beautiful lake, the road being bounded on the right by a perpen-dicular wall of rock of vast height, we entered a lovely valley. It was by no means so wild as many we have seen, but much prettier. The trees were more luxu-riant, the hills grass-covered, and the road bounded on the one hand by a rippling stream and on the other by fine fields of clover. Soon the road began to wind, and before us lay a magnificent fosse tumbling from a great rock that completely shut in the valley and which, to continue our journey, it was necessary that we should surmount. The road was well constructed. By a suc-cession of sloping zigzags it crossed the fall about half way up, affording a capital view of the upper volume of water, which flowed over a level tract of rock for some

distance before taking its final leap into the stream
below.   The upper fall is, I should think, about the
same height as the lower, and after crossing the flat in-
tervening land, the zigzag road again wriggles like a
snake up the steep rocks until at last it emerges on a
comparatively open district, through which flows the
now placid stream, which frequently makes large pools
from which are constantly springing great fishes.   We
were obliged to walk by an old path to the summit as,
owing to its great height and the length of constantly
ascending road required to gain it, it would have been
cruel to compel the ponies to haul a heap of lazy
tourists to the top.   However, we enjoyed our
climb.

We now traversed a park-like district, more English
in its appearance than any part of Norway we were as
yet acquainted with.   It was a delicious evening and,
truth to tell, we were, if anything, rather sorry when
after a drive of nearly twenty miles we passed through
the pretty village of Vossevangen and halted at the
door of Fleischer's Hotel.   J. C. Phythian, in his
"Scenes of Travel in Norway," is enthusiastic in his
praises of the establishment and its proprietor, and A.
W. Slack informs us that "Herr Fleischer is most
agreeable."   I can, even now, after so short an acquaintance, cordially echo their sentiments, for to-night
we find everything most comfortable, Fleischer one of
the jolliest little fellows imaginable, speaking English
well, and supper, oh ! wasn't it good ! By the bye, what
enormous appetites we have had since we came to the
"land of the midnight sun."   I declare, I despatch as
much as five ordinary mortals would in England.

July 5th.—Spent the day most enjoyably at Vossevangen.   Fleischer's Hotel is very prettily situated and
beautifully arranged.   Within a few yards of the entrance stretches a large lake bounded by hills covered,
for the most part, with healthy foliage, embowered
amid which are picturesque farms.   To the left, as I
look towards the glassy expanse from the verandah of
the hotel, lies Vossevangen, its quaint church spire

conspicuous above the surrounding buildings; and at my feet is a fine garden with lots of gooseberry bushes laden with fruit, whilst behind rises a mountain. These are the leading features in a delightful picture.

In the morning we had a most enjoyable row upon the placid waters of the lake.

We strolled through a thick fir forest to the river which flows near Vossevangen. We were much interested in the ferns and flowers which flourish here; and having played " dick, duck and drake " at the river for some time, we returned, had—well, I'll not tell you what and went to—never mind where.

July 6th.—Rose early and, in company with Mr. and Mrs. de Horne—most agreeable people, whom we have got to know since coming to Fleischer's, set out across the country to Gudvangen. A splendid drive! During one stage of the journey there were seventeen waterfalls in sight at once. After leaving Stalheim the road descends by a very long and winding route, from various points of which we obtained glorious views of two of the finest fosses imaginable, one in the right hand corner of the valley we were making for and the other occupying a similar position to the left. We often paused in our walk, for we had quitted our cars and carriole (I travelled in the latter, as usual, it being my favourite mode of conveyance) previous to commencing the descent, to admire the lovely wreaths as of purest snow which fell with a roar beneath us, the different streams uniting after a short course of loneliness, and forming a stream of rippling and many-hued, but greenish, water. Before us, to the left, on our entrance to the valley, rose, amid the many wild peaks that shot upwards in savage splendour, a gigantic dome-shaped rock. There it was, alone—for chasms spread around it completely isolating it; yet not alone, for on all sides, within a few yards, rose " the wildest forms and the most delicate outlines." It seemed to stand there as a monument to argue of " righteousness, temperance, and judgment "—to tell of the existence, Omnipotence, Omniscience, and Omnipresence of

Jehovah, and to ever resound with the honour of the glory of His great Name !

I declare, this drive almost equalled the one I endeavoured to describe through the Roms-dal. The rocks were, if anything, even grander than those over which I flew into such rhapsodies near Aak ; but there were fewer waterfalls to relieve the desolateness of the scene, and the clouds were now of a cold silver hue instead of being tipped with scintillating flashes of amber, as on the former occasion.

I had an excellent pony. Oh ! that there were such ponies in England as in Norway. Such willing, docile, enduring, and graceful little creatures—really, although I don't generally possess much attachment for the equine race, I was fascinated by the Norwegian specimens of it. My skyd was most obliging and spoke English well. A strapping nut-brown maid, rather pretty, acted as skyd for Mr. and Mrs. de H——. These "skyds" were remarkably kind to their beasts, never omitting to get out and walk if it were necessary to surmount a hill. I noticed that the aforesaid maid on such occasions walked by the side of the hereinbefore-mentioned skyd, and, moreover, methought they held loving converse together.

As we neared Gudvangen a tremendously lofty fall came in view. From a precipice 2,000 feet above the level of the sea it plunges in the form of a cluster of wriggling snow-white serpents, unbroken for 800 feet. Here it is intercepted by a ledge, and in tortuous beauty curls over the jagged rocks which intervene between the ledge and the river. The volume of water is not large, but the great height of the fall and the grandeur of the encircling mountains endow it with as much that is calculated to inspire awe as anything we have met with in Norway. Ziba Armitage describes this fosse as a myth, but he doubtless visited Gudvangen at an inopportune season.

We dined at a good "hotel" and then went on board the "Fjalir," a comfortable steamer plying between Bergen and the places on the Sogne Fjord. At five we sailed, the scenery being absolutely terrible in wonder.

Gudvangen is built at the end of the Naero Fjord, one of the finest branches of the Sogne, which is "an enormous fjord in plan resembling the skeleton of a tree, and running upwards of 120 English miles inland." The branches excel the body in grandeur. " Many are dark narrow lanes of water bent into reaches, which here and there expand to the size of lakes. Wooded precipices rise straight from the deep, and numerous cataracts roar down on all sides." The description I have quoted from " Murray " does not quite apply to the Naero, for the precipices are bare and bleak as those of the infernal regions, being utterly destitute of vegetation for the most part, save where sickly grass pines in melancholy between the sheltering sides of some friendly cleft. Castles impregnable, which one can well imagine to be crowded with grisly, spectral soldiery, were built, in my mind, amid the chaos of mountains.

In the evening the scenery got tamer, but was still beautiful. The sun set in a blaze of pinkish glory over the hill-tops, and through the gathering gloom we could descry a flame and a dense smoke on shore. The captain examined it through his glass, and the passengers expressed their opinions as to its cause, the general conjecture being that it was a house on fire!

At ten we anchored at Laerdalsören, where Mr. and Mrs. de H—— left us, and where the steamer remained until four the next morning,

July 7th,—When I was awoke by the noise which the " Fjalir " made as she again cleaved the waves. We were sailing until 11 p.m., having sighted the Justedal Glacier in the course of the day, when we reached Bergen. An old gentleman who had journeyed with us offered us accommodation for the night, but, on arriving at his abode, we found that several other visitors were already there, and that consequently there was no room for us. The good-natured old fellow then took us to the Hotel Scandinavi and said "Good night." We could not even here find comfortable apartments, as the best were occupied, so we made for the Hotel Nordstjernen, which had been recommended to us by Mr. Macreight, an Irish gentleman who had sailed with us from Gudvangen to Sögndal on the " Fjalir." Here we were soon installed most conveniently.

July 8th.—After breakfast, which was composed of twenty varieties of eatables, we went down to the fish market. A great number of boats were ranged along the quay full of fine fish, and a crowd of inhabitants were assembled, who brought great affairs as large as coal boxes to contain the fish they purchased. How cheap everything was! A few orer (an ore is equivalent to about the seventh of a penny) would purchase many a shovel-full of small mackerel, &c. Really, it was a very interesting sight, and I wish I could give you an adequate picture.

From here we walked to the castle, part of which is now used as a prison, the remainder being occupied by the commandant and the royal family when they visit Bergen. The soldiers' band was practising in one of the buildings overlooking a courtyard, where we sat for a long time listening to the pleasing strains of the musicians, who, I was afterwards told, rank among the finest in Europe. Passing through a lovely avenue we came to a kind of fort, where were ranged cannon and mortars, which were fired at intervals by a detachment of artillerymen. This occupation soon lost its charms, and we were then conducted through the castle, which was erected by Olaf Kyrre, the founder of the city, and was formerly the abode of those Norwegian kings who made Bergen their capital. The Walkendorff Tower is used as an armoury and contains hundreds of rifles, bayonets and swords. The different apartments are reached by means of a spiral staircase, opening on to the roof, from which we obtained a very good view of the town and harbour.

We returned to the hotel, I intent upon seeking repose, and Mr. Saxon and Harry, after a short rest, resuming their stroll. At about half-past one, as I lay in a very elegant position, my head and body upon the bed and my legs resting upon a chair, whilst my thoughts were of the " wreck of matter and the crash of the worlds," and their connection with quilts, blankets and fladbrod, or some such peculiar subject, I was surprised to hear voices strange yet familiar mingling with the well-known tones of Mr. Saxon and Harry, who, I presumed, for my semi-somnolence permitted me to reason thus far, had returned. But who the strangers were I couldn't think. I sprang up in a very untidy condition, entered the adjacent room, for we had two opening into each other, and, to my great surprise, was greeted by Mr. Palmer and his companion Mr. Pretty. It seems that they had just arrived in Bergen and were located at Holdt's.

In the afternoon I went to the Museum, a very handsome building. It is not open on Tuesday ; but on payment of 20 orer I was admitted. I should certainly advise all who find themselves in Bergen to visit the Museum, for it contains some most interesting objects. The zoological department is first-rate, there being numerous specimens of reindeer, bears, foxes, and other Norwegian animals ; elephants, giraffes, antelopes, seals, and birds and fishes in every variety. There are some huge skeletons, one, of a whale, being, as near as I could ascertain, ninety feet in length. Then there were the usual antiquities—as armour, furniture, china, apparel, coins, &c. I enjoyed the inspection of the innumerable curiosities immensely.

Having some time to spare I next strolled to the end of the promontory on which the principal part of Bergen is built, and which commands a grand view of the southern part of the city and the ships and boats which throng the harbour, while just at your feet stretches a sea of red tiles.

On my return I heard from Mr. Saxon and Harry, who had been to the Art Gallery, that the " Domino," the steamer on which we intended to sail for Hull on Thursday, would not reach Bergen until Saturday, as she had been sent to Trondhjem for a cargo of salmon. We were unanimous in our condemnation of the conduct of

Messrs. Thomas Wilson, Sons and Co., in shattering people's arrangements, and paying no regard to their own regulations. I believe they have a monopoly of the passenger traffic between England and Norway, and consequently do just as they like without caring for the inconvenience to which they may put others. Of course there may be extenuating circumstances of which I am unaware. If so, I trust my readers will consider them.

July 9th.—We breakfasted with a most distinguished-looking old gentleman and his wife, who is young, pretty, and has a pair of wondrously fascinating blue eyes. They were both most agreeable. Mr. Saxon had a warm political argument with the gentleman, who is, apparently, a strong Radical, whilst Mr. Saxon is a Conservative. Afterwards we walked down to the offices of Wilson and Co. to ascertain if there were any more news of the "Domino." We received a negative reply to our enquiries. Having examined the fishing-boats that were moored in the vicinity we returned through a churchyard. Beneath the church, opening by means of wooden gates on a lawn, were several tombs, containing numerous elaborate coffins. I began to muse upon the scene. Before and around me were the remains of men of like passions with ourselves. They had once trod these busy streets and mingled with their fellow men. Their hopes, their joys, their good impulses had once asserted sway and made themselves felt in the circle amid which they moved. But now, the hearts that once bounded with rapture, or beat mournfully in dismay, were silent for ever ; and the forms that, perhaps erect and beautiful, had once excited the admiration of humanity were "mouldering in the grave." And what had been accomplished by their existence ? Had they done their duty in that state of life unto which it had pleased God to call them ? Had they been determined opponents of fraud, injustice, cruelty, meanness, and crime ? Had they devoted their lives to the service of the human race and ever aimed to promote its aggrandizement ? Had they, during their earthly career, the consciousness of their Maker's smile resting upon them, and were their spirits now waiting to enter the paradise of the blest ? Or had they spent their strength for naught, and lived out their threescore years and ten without a thought, save that of self ; with hearts hard as iron, and with a deaf ear to the wails of misery which echoed around them ? Mayhap some had died to the satisfaction of their nearest acquaintance, and would soon be ushered into the unseen world of terrors to answer for the deeds done in the body. But others, let us hope, had fallen peaceably asleep in hope of a joyful resurrection, mourned by thousands to whom they had administered comfort, and counsel, and love, and who now found glorious consolation in the confident knowledge that they were " not lost, but gone before." Oh ! to live, not useless lives, but lives which make the world nobler, and braver, and better ; and to die happy deaths, whilst amid sorrowing tears hundreds whisper, " He was a good man ! " Life is worth living thus ! May I and all my readers, when our spirits have fled from our decomposed ashes, merit the grand eulogium, " He was a good man ! " and exchange our earthly inheritance for that which is incorruptible and undefiled, and that fadeth not away !

As we were returning to the hotel we were rather astonished to meet a gentleman whose acquaintance we had made on board the "Fjalir," Mr. Macreight, and who, as the reader will remember, left us at Sögndal. He informed us that he had just arrived from thence and that during his stay there he had been fed on " fish and pancakes."

The Queen's (not Victoria) sister came this morning, her arrival being celebrated by a tremendous discharge of cannon.

In the afternoon we sailed up the lakes which lave the eastern end of Bergen, on board the small steamer, "Strömmen." We passed some very fine country seats and, during the return sail, had a magnificent view of the city.

In the evening I was destined to behold the most
sublime sight I ever witnessed.   Mr. Saxon had gone
to the public gardens soon after supper to meet Messrs.
P—— and P——, whilst Harry and I adjourned to a
balcony, where we were soon seated chatting gaily.
Suddenly we noticed a lovely pink hue pervading the
sky above the lakes, and, the next instant, Mr. Saxon,
in a state of great excitement, rushed up the stairs and
informed us that he wished us to go with him to the
gardens to view a gorgeous sunset.   We went, and
never shall I forget the vision of glory which there burst
upon us.   The band was playing a beautiful air as we
entered, and its harmonious strains floated softly upon
the still night air.   By-the-bye, it was the same band
we had heard at the castle.   The gardens, which are
tastefully laid out with trees, walks, &c., were thronged
with the grandees of Bergen.   Ladies, with lovely faces
and figures of nymph - like grace, sauntered up and
down laughing musically, or chatting in voices sweet as
the tinkling of silver bells.   Stalwart youths paraded
the well-kept paths, their faces beaming with delight as
they acknowledged the fascinating smiles of their
female friends.   Everyone seemed pleased—it was like
a great pleasure gathering unmarred by the sounds of
strife.   Everyone seemed to know everyone, and on
all hands cordial greetings were constantly inter-
changed.

Towards the east, running between two picturesque
mountains, were two lakes, whose waters almost laved
the edge of the park.   From summit to summit
stretched an arch of prismatic colour of more than
ordinary brilliance and every moment growing brighter.
Within the glorious arch lay, first, a grove of the most
verdant trees.   Then came the calm waters of the lakes
and, covering the mountain sides, fine mansions and
elaborate buildings surrounded by exquisite foliage.
Beyond, the valley grew shadowy and more shadowy
until at the horizon, in a charming violet hue, it mingled
with the sky.   The picture, in itself lovely, was bathed
in ethereal light.   Flashing pink blended with gorgeous

amber and seemed to flood the valley with radiance
more than natural. It were easy to imagine the rainbow the archway by which to seek entrance to the
palaces not made with hands; and the blaze of pink,
amber and orange light gradually softening into the
most delicate violet might well represent the first
dawning of the light which proceeds, not from sun,
nor moon, nor stars, nor candles,—for none of these
are needed to illumine the place where Jehovah
dwelleth, — but from Him, the Father of Lights,
Who hath declared " that there shall be no night
there!"

Brighter and brighter grew the scene, and methought
my Maker smiled as each succeeding and superseding
flash threw its rays beneath the grandific archway. All
the darkness was banished from my spirit and my heart
o'erflowed with gratitude to the Giver of every good and
perfect gift as, fascinated, I basked in His smile of
splendour, and tears rose, uncalled, to my eyes as I
thought of my utter unworthiness, my irreverence, my
profanity, my heinous sin.

If a scene like this would not convince the most confirmed atheist of the fallacy of his ideas he must indeed
be a Didymus beyond conviction, and from my soul I
pity him.

Beyond the archway every window shone like bur-
nished gold, and cloudlets, purple-hued, floated through
the pink light to blush into yet greater loveliness
beneath its magic glow. Behind us other clouds of
the most flashing crimson were congregated in shapely
crowds. In whatever direction we turned sublimity
met our gaze—look which way we would, we beheld
the pageantry of the King of kings. Gradually the
rainbow expired and like a dream the light which had
streamed beneath it passed from its shelter to steal
behind the mountain to the right of us and in glory
die.

And now, having beheld God's majesty and goodness
in earth, air, sea and sky can we do better than fervently
and adoringly quote Sir R. Grant's noble song of thanks-

giving ? Nay, surely not ! for the mighty mountains, the curling mists, the azure heavens, the beautiful billows and the ten thousand other wonders of Norway which I have tried to describe to you are, you will all agree, worthy, well worthy, of his noble Te Deum :

> " Oh ! worship the King,
>   All glorious above !
> And gratefully sing
>   His power and His love ;
> Our Shield and Defender,
>   The Ancient of days,
> Pavilioned in splendour,
>   And girded with praise.

> " Oh ! tell of His might,
>   Oh ! sing of His grace,
> Whose robe is the light,
>   Whose canopy space ;
> Whose chariots of wrath
>   Deep thunderclouds form,
> And dark is His path
>   On the wings of the storm.

> " The earth with its store
>   Of wonders untold,
> Almighty ! Thy power
>   Hath founded of old ;
> Hath stablished it fast
>   By a changeless decree,
> And round it hath cast,
>   Like a mantle, the sea.

> " Thy bountiful care
>   What tongue can recite ?
> It breathes in the air,
>   It shines in the light ;
> It streams from the hills,
>   It descends to the plain,
> And sweetly distils
>   In the dew and the rain.

" Frail children of dust,
    And feeble as frail,
In Thee do we trust,
    Nor find Thee to fail ;
Thy mercies, how tender,
    How firm to the end !
Our Maker, Defender,
    Redeemer and Friend !

" Oh ! measureless might !
    Ineffable love !
While angels delight
    To hymn Thee above,
The humbler creation,
    Though feeble their lays,
With true adoration
    Shall lisp to Thy praise."

The band was discoursing the sweet airs in " La Fille
du Regiment," and hundreds walked the park in eager
tones discussing the enchanting view which had just
disappeared. Suddenly a great shower came on and
we all rushed to the shelter of the trees. The rain soon
subsided and we resumed our stroll. We met with
Messrs. P—— and P——, and were told by Mr. P——y
that an inhabitant of Bergen had just stated that *he'd*
never seen a sunset to equal this before, though he had
spent the greater part of his life in Norway.

We also met one of the University fellows we had got
to know at the Victoria, Christiania.

On our return we ascertained from Mr. M—— that
the gentleman and lady with whom we had breakfasted were Ole Bull, the great violinist, and his
wife.

I was deeply interested by the information, for I was
once designated " Ole Bull Arthur " by some particular
friends, and long went by that name.

Ole Bull was born at the " Swan " apothecary's shop,
which we have several times seen since we came to
Bergen. The chemists' shops in Norway always have
a sign, like our English inns.

July 10*th.*—Went out fishing on the bay with our
Irish friend, Mr. M——, and, after about two hours'
labour, managed to catch one whiting and dozens of
mussels, which latter, however, clung to the posts by
the quay in countless multitudes, and were used by us
as bait.

Speaking of mussels reminds me of a tale told
by Mr. Saxon concerning an old fellow who was
very unwell, and whose physician ordered him champagne and oysters. Some time afterwards the doctor
called again and noticed that his patient was much
better.

" Did you give him what I told you " ? he asked of
the wife.

" Well, no sir! we found champagne and oysters
rather expensive ; but we gave him plenty of pop and
cockles."

There was another pretty sunset, which we viewed
from the elevated part of the promontory.

July 11*th.*—In the course of the day Harry and I
visited the Art Gallery, which contains some fine paintings, principally landscape.

Again the sun set in a blaze of glory, tinging the banks
of clouds which floated in an ethereal sky with colour
infinitely richer than the most skilled artist could depict
—the most fertile brain conceive. We watched its
triumphal departure from the castle, and afterwards
went to the park, where we met Messrs. P—— and
P——, who were, as usual, full of wit, and our University
friends, who, we learn, sail with us in the " Domino "
on Saturday, one of them hoping to be in time to play
in the cricket match, Eton *v.* Harrow.

July 12*th.*—Our sojourn at the Hotel Nordstjernen
terminated by our embarkation at noon. This hotel is
most comfortable—indeed, I like it better than any I
have seen in Norway—and I can confidently recommend
it to tourists. The charges are very moderate, and the
attention all that can be desired. One thing is rather

peculiar in connection with it, though. The proprietor is always, or nearly always, smoking, and
upon being seen by a customer generally vanishes
mysteriously.

The " Domino," to my mind, is by no means so comfortable as the " Hero," and we missed the friendly face
of " John Smith."

Soon after twelve we sailed from Bergen, to my regret,
for of all the towns I have visited I like it the best, and,
contrary to my anticipations, have enjoyed our four days'
stay immensely.

I need not describe the voyage to Stavanger, where
we arrived at 10 p.m., having passed Haugesund and
Kopervik. At Haugesund " a granite obelisk, erected
1872, stands near *the gravestone of Harold Haarfager*,
the first king of all Norway. At least, so it is called,
and the popular belief here is that he was buried there.
But this appears doubtful, as by another account the
place of his interment is stated to have been ' one of his
manors in Drontheim ; ' and that ' near the spot a
magnificent heathen temple was erected, which was
standing in the days of Snorro.' "

A host of people assembled on the quay at Stavanger
to meet the " Domino," and for some time there was a
scene of great activity. The town, in the dim light,
looked very picturesque. It is situated on the north-
east side of a large promontory in Stavanger Fjord, and
commands a fine view of the Fjord and the range of
mountains in the distance extending to the Hardanger
range. It contains about 18,000 inhabitants, and derives
its importance from the herring fishery, the yearly catch
of which averages between 300,000 and 400,000 barrels.
It is a very ancient city, and was a bishopric before the
foundation of Christiansand. The Cathedral, next to
that of Trondhjem, is considered to be the best specimen
of the architecture of the Middle Ages in Norway. It
has undergone a complete restoration. " The nave is
Norman—the rest Gothic of the thirteenth century, of
the early English character."

July 13*th.*—After breakfast, during which we were
informed that it had been very rough in the night, I had
a long stroll on deck with an American gentleman,
whom we had got to know at the Hotel Nordstjernen.
Gradually the wind rose, and there was every appearance of an impending storm. Harry soon succumbed
and returned his breakfast, though not in its original
state. Now *I* had determined not to be sick on any
account, and, the wind still rising, as the best pre-
ventive I entered my berth and commenced reading
"The King's Own." The rain now came down in
torrents, and the ship rolled fearfully—so much so
that I felt rather unwell, and deeming my present
situation the safest, remained there without dinner.
Tea-time came, but Harry and I contented ourselves
with biscuit. What got over me was that no one else
seemed to be ill, and Mr. Saxon had been on deck all
day.

At eight I resolved to undress and go to sleep, if
possible. I jumped from my berth and speedily
divested myself of my garments. "Now," thought I,
"I'm a great man! I shall manage to avoid sea-
sickness." I sprang up again, but, experiencing a
strange sensation, I tried to conquer it and lay down.
Alas! 'twas useless! The next instant I found that I
was no better than anyone else, for, "woe is me!" I
am sick! Fortunately it was a very slight attack, and I
now felt much better.

A dense fog had arisen and, on opening the porthole,
I found that it was only possible to see a few yards
ahead of the steamer. Consequently the horn was
blown every few minutes, to our great discomfort, for it
makes a hideous din. Mr. Saxon came to bed soon
afterwards, and then we found that we were not the only
sufferers from *mal de mer.* He himself had been
perched in the smoke-room all day, feeling very seedy.
One of the University fellows had fallen in a heap at
the top of the staircase and lain there for three hours,
notwithstanding the solicitations of his friends, justify-
ing himself by saying that it was the most comfortable

place he could find. Another gentleman, who reclined in a corner of the smoke-room full length, plaintively murmured :

" I'm very un'appy ! "

" Why ? " was the query.

" Because I want to go down below very badly, and if I do, some one will take my place ! "

His friends promised to reserve the corner, and he then disappeared, and, as Mr. Saxon told us, "has not since been heard of."

It appears that eight had sat down to dinner, all of whom save the Captain and the American gentleman speedily made their exit.

I had almost omitted to mention that the wife and daughters who had been committed to our care by a gentleman on board " Hardangeren," as I have herein-before stated, sailed, according to his words, for England on the " Domino, " and very agreeable we found them.

July 14*th.*—The storm had almost subsided when we awoke, and after breakfast the passengers all seemed to have recovered their wonted happiness. We soon sighted land, and at eleven o'clock were steaming past the Spurn Lights.

Much as I have enjoyed my visit to Norway, and favourably as I am impressed with it, I felt glad to again sight the shores of Old England, which, with all its faults, I love. With Scott I can say most earnestly :—

" Breathes there the man with soul so dead,
　Who never to himself hath said,
　This is my own, my native land !
　Whose heart hath ne'er within him burned
　As home his footsteps he hath turned,
　From wandering on a foreign strand ?
　If such there breathe, go, mark him well !
　For him no minstrel raptures swell !
　High though his titles, proud his name,

" Boundless his wealth as wish can claim :
Despite those titles, power and pelf,
The wretch, concentred all in self—
Living, shall forfeit fair renown,
And doubly dying, shall go down
To the vile dust, from whence he sprung,
Unwept, unhonoured, and unsung."

We disembarked, dined at the Royal Station Hotel,
bade our many friends " good bye," entered a train, were
whirled towards Warrington, and, at about eight o'clock,
drew up at the platform of the Central Station, to be
greeted like conquering heroes by our friends, and to
drive home in state, there to astonish all with whom we
came in contact by our wondrous stories of travel in
" the land of the midnight sun."

*   *   *   *   *   *   *

And now I must conclude.   Has my visit to Norway
been useless ?   Nay, verily! for it has taught me much
that it is well for me to know; has shown me that the
English are not the only worthy race upon the earth;
that the Norwegians are not, as I had long supposed,
in a state of semi-barbarity; that we, with all our
bravery, and wisdom, and goodness, are, in many
respects, inferior to them.   It has clearly demonstrated
the fact that I ought not to look down upon any one
until I have sufficient cause for so doing; and has made
me value politeness, generosity, nobility of soul, and
every manly virtue, even more than was my wont; has
been the means of instructing me much in geography,
in geology, in zoology, in history, and in poetry; has
filled my mind with visions of beauty which in dark
hours will flash with lustre in my memory, and thrill me
with purest joy ; has added considerably, I trust, to my
fund of common sense ; has imparted increased vigour
to my body, which I hope will prove enduring; and
lastly, and best of all, having in Norway beheld
wherever I went, whether by carriole, by car, by

steamer, by boat, by rail, or on foot, the impress of the Creator's hand, I have been led to believe, more earnestly than ever, that notwithstanding the jeers of sceptics, the blasphemies of infidels, the damnable arguments of atheists, to believe most conscientiously, adoringly, and, I trust, lastingly, that "the Lord Omnipotent reigneth."

FINIS.